arcola
theatre

The Painter

by Rebecca Lenkiewicz

First performed at Arcola Theatre on 12 January 2011

Arcola Theatre is funded by the Arts Council England

Supported by
**ARTS COUNCIL
ENGLAND**

Arcola Theatre
24 Ashwin Street
Dalston, London E8 3DL

Arcola Theatre presents

The Painter

by Rebecca Lenkiewicz

Cast
in order of appearance

WILLIAM TURNER	Jim Bywater
TURNER	Toby Jones
SARAH DANBY	Niamh Cusack
JENNY COLE	Denise Gough
MARY MARSHALL TURNER	Amanda Boxer
HEREFORD / MAN	Ian Midlane

Production Team

Director	Mehmet Ergen
Set and Costumes	Ben Stones
Lighting	Emma Chapman
Music and Sound	Adrienne Quartly
Production Manager	Stuart Farnell
Stage Manager	Martha Mamo
Assistant Director	Katharine Armitage
Assistant Stage Manager	Amelia Hankin
Fight Director	Chris Jenkins
Press	Jennifer Reynolds for Target Live (020 3372 0950)
Production Photography	Simon Annand www.simonannand.com

Thanks to:
Nina Segal at Donmar Warehouse,
Mela Yerka (www.melayerka.com),
Almeida Theatre.

arcola
theatre

Over the last 10 years Arcola Theatre has taken thousands of theatregoers on a theatrical journey by producing and presenting some of the most diverse and challenging work for the London stage. We have presented plays and opera that have rarely seen the light of day as well as revisiting more contemporary playwrights and presenting the finest international work. Arcola Theatre has championed new writers and emerging directors and offered a continuing platform with which to continue their journey. We look forward to continuing the journey at our new home in Ashwin Street.

For Arcola Theatre

Artistic Director	Mehmet Ergen
Executive Producer	Leyla Nazli
Executive Director	Ben Todd
General Manager	Catherine Thornborrow

Youth and Community

Projects Manager	Owen Calvert-Lyons
Projects Assistant	Nadia Gasper

Sustainability

Projects Manager	Feimatta Conteh

Marketing

Marketing Manager	Barry Wilson
Marketing Assistants	Selvi Akyildiz, Venessa Howell

Technical

Technical Manager	David Salter
Technical Assistant	Amelia Hankin

Finance

Finance Manager	Helen Hillman
Finance Assistant	Amanda Koch-Schick

Front of House and Box Office

Managers	Charlotte Croft, Harriet Warnock
Box Office Assistants	Archie Backhouse, Stephen McCann, Jacklene Silwano
Bar Supervisor	Haydar Koyel
Bar Staff	Pauline Hoare

Arcola Energy

Associate Technologist	Matthew Venn
Engineers	Simon Mylius, Rajvinder Malhi
Marketing Assistant	Amanda Bicott

Arcola Theatre Ambassadors

Archie Backhouse, Rowan Thomas Cliff, Jodiese Davis,
Ella Garrard, PJ Mathison, Jake Morgan-Stead, Esme Kirk,
Connor Sanderson, Zehra Yas

With thanks to all our dedicated volunteers and interns

Cast

in alphabetical order

Amanda Boxer (Mary Marshall Turner)

Theatre includes: *The Prisoner of Second Avenue* (Vaudeville Theatre); *Cling to Me Like Ivy* (Birmingham Rep / Tour); *Many Roads to Paradise* (Finborough / Jermyn St); *The Last Days Of Judas Iscariot* (Almeida); *The Pain and the Itch, The Strip* (both Royal Court); *An Ideal Husband, The Rivals* (both Theatre Clywd); *Dis-Orientations* (Riverside Studios); *The Arab Israeli Cookbook* (Gate Theatre / Tricycle); *A Small Family Business* (West Yorkshire Playhouse); *The Destiny of Me* (Finborough); *Macbeth* (Arcola Theatre); *The Graduate* (Gielgud); *The Yiddish Queen Lear* (Bridewell); *Iphigenia at Aulis* (Southwark Playhouse); *A Touch of the Poet* (Young Vic / Comedy Theatre); *The House of Bernarda Alba* (The Globe); *All My Sons, The Merchant of Venice, Othello, The Importance of Being Earnest* (all Young Vic); *Come Blow Your Horn, The Fall Guy, The Misanthrope, Absurd Person Singular, Present Laughter* (all Royal Exchange); *Secret Rapture, Death and the Maiden* (Library Theatre Manchester). Best Actress in the 1992 London Fringe Awards for Martha in *Strange Snow*.

Television includes: *Bodies 3, The Shell Seakers, Casualty, Trial and Retribution, Chalk, Ruth Rendell Mysteries, Unnatural Pursuits, Inspector Alleyn Mysteries, Cider with Rosie, Goodbye My Love, In Suspicious Circumstances.*

Films include: *Malice in Wonderland, Chatroom, United 93, Les Poupées Russes, Saving Private Ryan.*

Jim Bywater (William Turner)

Theatre includes: *Three Sisters* (Lyric Hammersmith); *Uncle Vanya* (Young Vic); *Ghosts, Lady from the Sea, An Enemy of the People, A Midsummer Night's Dream* (all Arcola Theatre Theatre); *Only When I Laugh* (Arcola Theatre and Tour); *Chasing the Moment* (Arcola Theatre/National Studio/Southwark Playhouse and Israel Tour); *The Trackers of Oxyrhynccus* (National Theatre, Scandinavia and Austria Tours); *The Merchant of Venice , Two Gentlemen of Verona* (both Shakespeare's Globe and New York); *Dracula, Blitz, The Importance of Being Earnest, Face, Oh What a Lovely War, Sleeping Beauty, The Tempest, Mother Goose* (all Queen's Theatre, Hornchurch); *Oedipus Tyrranos, Macbeth* (both Battersea Arts Centre).

Television includes: *Coronation Street, Dalziel and Pascoe, Accidental Death of an Anarchist.*

Niamh Cusack (Sarah Danby)

Theatre includes: *Women, Power & Politics* (Tricycle Theatre); *Andersen's English* (Hampstead / UK Tour); *Dancing at Lughnasa* (The Old Vic); *Portrait of a Lady* (Theatre Royal Bath); *Crestfall* (Theatre503); *The Enchantment* (National Theatre); *The Way of the World* (Northampton); *Ghosts* (Gate Theatre); *Mammals* (Bush Theatre); *Merchant of Venice* (Chichester); *Breathing Corpses* (Royal Court Theatre); *His Darks Materials* (National Theatre); *As You Like It, Romeo + Juliet, Othello* (all RSC); *Three Sisters* (Gate Theatre / Royal Court).

Television includes: *Midsummer Murders, Fallen Angel, Little Bird, Loving You, Miss Marple – 4.50 from Paddington, Too Good to be True.*

Film includes: *Hereafter, The Closer You Get, Playboys, The Kid, Paris by Night, Lucky Sunil, Fools of Fortune.*

Denise Gough (Jenny Cole)

Theatre includes: *The Plough and the Stars* (Abbey Theatre); *Jesus Hopped the A Train* (Trafalgar Studios); *The Birds* (Gate Theatre, Dublin); *Six Characters in Search of an Author* (West End / Chichester); *The Grouch* (West Yorkshire Playhouse); *Someone Else's Shoes* (Soho Theatre); *Everything is Illuminated* (Hampstead Theatre); *Oh Go My Man* (Royal Court Theatre); *As You Like It* (Wyndhams, West End); *By the Bog of the Cats* (Wyndhams, West End); *The Kindess of Strangers* (Liverpool Everyman).

Film includes: *The Kid, Robin Hood, Desire, Lecture 21, The Shooting of Thomas Hurndall.*

Television includes: *Casualty, The Bill, Silent Witness, Waking the Dead, Messiah, Inspector Lynley Mysteries.*

Toby Jones (Turner)

Theatre includes: *Every Good Boy Deserves Favour* (National Theatre); *Parlour Song* (Almeida); *Dumb Waiter and other Pinter Pieces* (Trafalgar Studios); *The Play What I Wrote* (New York / West End – Olivier Award Best Supporting Actor); *The Nativity* (Young Vic).

Film Includes: *Captain America, My Week with Marilyn, Tinker, Tinker, Soldier, Spy, The Rite, Christopher and His Kind, Harry Potter and the Deathly Hallows, What's Wrong with Virginia, Your Highness, Sex, Drugs & Rock n Roll, Tin Tin, Creation, W, Frost/Nixon, City of Ember, St Trinians, The Mist, Night Watching, Amazing Grace, Infamous, The Painted Veil, Mrs Henderson Presents, Ladies in Lavender, Finding Neverland, Harry Potter and the Chamber of Secrets.*

Television includes: *Doctor Who, Mo, 10 Days to War, The Old Curiosity Shop, The Harlot's Progress, Elizabeth 1, The Way We Live Now.*

Ian Midlane (Hereford, Man)

Theatre includes: *The Cradle Will Rock* (Arcola Theatre); *Dr Faustus* (Royal Exchange, Manchester); *Anthony & Cleopatra* (Nuffield Theatre); *Nineteen Eighty-four* (Royal Exchange); *The Rivals* (Theatre Royal Bath – tour); *My Own Show* (Stephen Joseph Theatre); *Humble Boy* (Manchester Library Theatre); *Thirteenth Night* (Southwark Playhouse); *Measure for Measure, Macbeth, I Can Get It For You Wholesale* (all Arcola Theatre).

Television includes: *The Sarah Jane Adventures: Revenge of the Slitheen* (BBC); *Messiah IV : The Harrowing* (BBC/Paramount); *Doctors* (BBC); *Wire in the Blood 4* (Coastal Productions); *Fingersmith* (Sally Head Productions); *My Dad's the Prime Minister* (BBC); *Hunter* (BBC); *The Last Detective* (Meridian); *Manhunt* (BBC); *The Bill* (Talkback/Thames).

Creatives

Rebecca Lenkiewicz (Playwright)

For the stage: *The Lioness* (Tricycle); *The Typist* (Sky Arts); *Stars Over Kabul* (NYT/Traverse); *That Almost Unnameable Lust* (Clean Break / Soho Theatre); *Ghosts* (Ibsen adaptation – Arcola Theatre / ATC); *Her Naked Skin* (National Theatre); *Faeries* (Linbury Studio ROH); *An Enemy of the People* (Ibsen adaptation – Arcola Theatre); *Justitia* (Sadler's Wells); *Invisible Mountains* (National Theatre Education tour); *Blue Moon Over Poplar* (NYT/Soho Theatre); *The Soldier's Tale, 24 Hour Plays* (Old Vic); *Shoreditch Madonna* (Soho Theatre); *The Night Season* (National Theatre); *Soho - A Tale of Table Dancers* (Pleasance Edinburgh – Fringe First/Israel Tour/Arcola Theatre). Rebecca is currently under commission to the National Theatre and Manhattan Theatre Club, New York.

Radio plays: *Blue Moon Over Poplar, Caravan of Desire* (BBC), *Fighting for Words* (BBC).

Mehmet Ergen (Director)

Founder and Artistic Director of the Arcola Theatre; Founder and Artistic Director of the Talimhane Theatre in Istanbul; Co-founder and the first Artistic Director of the Southwark Playhouse (1993–1999). Founder of the new writing festival: Oyun Yaz.

Directing work includes: *Dumb Show* by Joe Penhall, *Afterplay* by Brian Friel, *Noises Off* by Michael Frayn, *Lieutenant of Inishmore, Pillowman* by Martin McDonagh, *The Betrayal, Ashes to Ashes, One for the Road* by Harold Pinter, *The Shape of Things* by Neil LaBute, *Fool for Love* by Sam Shepard, *The Nest* by Kroetz, *Much Ado About Nothing* and *King Lear* by W. Shakespeare, *Roots* by Arnold Wesker, *Of Mice and Men* by John Steinbeck, *The Protagonist* by Georg Kaiser, *In the Jungle of the Cities, Informer, Exception and the Rule* by Bertold Brecht, *Mandragola* by Machievelli.

For Arcola: *An Enemy of the People* by Ibsen, *Silver Birch House* by Leyla Nazli, *Chasing the Moment* by Jack Shepherd, *The Plebeians Rehearse the*

Uprising by Günter Grass, *Jitterbug* by Bonnie Greer, *A Midsummer Night's Dream* and *Macbeth* by W. Shakespeare (both with Jack Shepherd).

Operas and Musicals include: *The Cradle Will Rock* by Marc Blitzstein, *Seven Deadly Sins* by Brecht / Weill, *I Can Get It For You Wholesale* by J Weidman / Harold Rome (all for the Arcola Theatre), *Dorian* (Arts Theatre, West End), *Treemonisha* by Scott Joplin, *Lost in the Stars* by Kurt Weill (both at BAC).

Translations include works by Ibsen, Pinter, Shepard, LaBute, McDonagh and Enda Walsh.

Ben Stones (Set and Costumes)

Ben trained in stage design at Central Saint Martins College of Art and Design and went on to win a Linbury prize commission to design *Paradise Lost* for Rupert Goold.

Designs include: *Creditors* (Donmar Warehouse, Harvey Theatre BAM New York); *Kiss Of The Spider Woman* (Donmar Warehouse, National Tour); *Lower Ninth* (Donmar Trafalgar season); *No Idea* (Improbable Theatre at Young Vic); *Paradise Lost* (Headlong Theatre); *Beautiful Thing* (Sound Theatre, Leicester Square); *Humble Boy, Paradise Lost, Someone Who'll Watch Over Me, Just Between Ourselves* (Theatre Royal Northampton); *The Arab Israeli Cookbook* (Tricycle Theatre*); The Mighty Boosh, Mitchell and Webb Live!, Pappys Fun Club* (Phil McIntyre national tour); *The Vegemite Tales* (The Venue Leicester Sq); *When Five Years Pass* (Arcola Theatre); *The Herbal Bed, The Real Thing* (both Salisbury Playhouse); *Romeo and Juliet* (Shakespeare's Globe); *My Mother Said I Never Should* (Watford Palace); *My Dad's a Birdman* (Sheffield Crucible); *Speaking in Tongues* (Duke of Yorks, West End); *Crocodile* (Frank McGuinness premiere for Sky Arts); *Ingredient X* (Royal Court Theatre); *Doctor Faustus, Taste of Honey, Salt* (Royal exchange Manchester); *Inheritance* (Live Theatre Newcastle); *An Enemy of the People* (Sheffield Crucible).

Emma Chapman (Lighting)

Emma trained at Bristol Old Vic Theatre School.

Theatre credits in 2010 include: *Blowing* (Cambridge and tour); *The Maddening Rain* (Old Red Lion); Frantic Assembly at artsdepot; The Young Vic Schools' Theatre Festival; *Lulu* (Gate); *The Comedians* (Bolton Octagon); *Summerfolk* (Guildhall School); *Wet Weather Cover* (King's Head and Arts Theatre).

Earlier productions: *The Hostage* (Southwark Playhouse); *Public Property* (Trafalgar Studios); *The Spanish Tragedy* (Arcola Theatre); *The Ones That Flutter* (Theatre 503); *The Mountaintop* (Theatre 503 and Trafalgar Studios); *The Lifesavers* (Theatre 503 and Mercury Theatre, Colchester); *50 Ways to Leave your Lover at Christmas* (The Bush); *You Can See The Hills* (Studio, Manchester Royal Exchange and Young Vic); *Cherry Docs* (Kings Head Theatre); *Romeo and Juliet* (Middle Temple Hall); *Mules* (Young Vic); *Semi-Monde* (Guildhall School of Music and Drama); *The Good Soul of Szechuan, Señora Carrar's Rifles* (both Young People's Participation Programme, Young Vic); *Some Kind of Bliss* (Trafalgar Studios); *Closer* (Royal & Derngate, Northampton); *Not a Game For Boys* (Library Theatre, Manchester); *The Importance of Being Earnest* (Derby Playhouse); *Bash: Latterday Plays*

(Trafalgar Studios); *The Musical of Musicals, Beautiful Thing* (both Sound Theatre); *Richard III* (Cambridge Arts Theatre); *The Pied Piper* (Opera North); *Phaedra's Love* (Bristol Old Vic and The Barbican); *Smilin' Through* (Birmingham Rep & Contact Theatre, Manchester); *Twelfth Night* (Associate LD, English Touring Theatre); *Attempts On Her Life* (BAC); *High Society* (Aberystwyth Arts Centre & Swansea Grand).

In preparation: *Carmen* (Royal Northern College); *Bus Stop* (Stoke and Scarborough); *The Machine Gunners* (Polka Theatre); *Dangerous Corner* (Bury St Edmunds); *Così fan Tutte* (Royal College of Music).

www.emmachapman.co.uk

Adrienne Quartly (Music and Sound)

For Arcola Theatre: *Torn, Enemy of the People, Silver Birch House, Last Waltz Season, Bintou.*

Other theatre includes: *Miss Julie* (Katie Mitchell at Schaübuhne, Berlin); *Chekov in Hell* (Drum, Plymouth); *Stockholm* (Frantic Assembly/Sydney Theatre Company); *The Container* (Young Vic); *Here Lies Mary Spindler, Thomas Hobbes* (both RSC); *365* (National Theatre of Scotland); *93.2FM* (Royal Court Theatre); *Woyzeck* (St Ann's Warehouse, New York); *Reykjavik* (Shams, Edinburgh 10); *My Zinc Bed, Private Fears and Public Places, Just Between Ourselves* (all Royal and Derngate, Northampton); *The Grand Guignol* (Drum Plymouth); *The Fastest Clock in the Universe* (Hampstead); *Mrs Reynolds and the Ruffian* (Watford Palace); *My Real War* (Trafalgar Studios); *Small Change* (Sherman Cymru); *Balloon Gardener* (Circo Ridiculoso); *Hysteria* (Inspector Sands); *Tejas Verdes* (Gate Theatre); *Playing For Time, A Touch of the Sun* (both Salisbury Playhouse); *Jarman Garden* (Riverside Studios).

Composer on *Thomas Hobbes* (RSC); *Lighter than Air* (Circo Ridiculoso); *Faustus/School for Scandal/Volpone/Duchess Malfi* (Stage on Screen/ Greenwich); *A Christmas Carol* (Sherman Cymru).

www.adriennequartly.com.

Stuart Farnell (Production Manager)

After studying theatre at York St John University, Stuart went on to work in the York Theatre Royal as a casual stage technician. He went on to tour with Pilot Theatre as Technical Manager on shows such as *Lord of the Flies, East is East, Sing Yer heart Out For The Lads* and *Fungus the Bogey Man.*

After moving to London, Stuart worked as a Deputy Technical Manager at Hampstead Theatre for a year and half and as Deputy Technical Manager for Regents Park Open Air Theatre for the 2010 Summer Season.

Stuart currently owns and runs a small but busy production company called Upstaged Scenery, which he set up in September this year. Upstaged Scenery has worked on projects at Arcola, Soho Theatre and Drill Hall Theatre to name a few.

Martha Mamo (Stage Manager)

Martha completed a postgraduate course in stage management at the Royal Welsh College of Music and Drama in 2005. Theatre credits include: *Ivan and the Dogs* (Soho Theatre); *Pieces of Vincent, Light Shining in Buckinghamshire* (both Arcola Theatre); *Kursk* (Fuel, Sound & Fury, Young Vic); *Kreutzer Sonata, Breathing Irregular* (both Gate Theatre); *Duet For One* (Almeida); *A Miracle, The Pride* (both Royal Court Theatre); *A2K* (Celebrations Global); *Chess in Concert* (Heartache Production); *Presidents Holiday* (Hampstead Theatre); *Parade* (Donmar Warehouse); *One Flew Over The Cuckoo's Nest* (Nimax); *The Changeling* (Cheek By Jowl); *Aladdin* (Old Vic); *The Bull, Flowerbed* (both Fabulous Beast); *Julius Caesar* (BITE); *Pam Ann Wants You, How to Lose Friends And Alienate People* (both Soho Theatre).

Katharine Armitage (Assistant Director)

Katharine recently graduated from the University of Manchester. She previously worked as Assistant Director on *The Cradle Will Rock* (Arcola Theatre). Directing includes: *The Pillowman* (University of Manchester); *The Love of the Nightingale* (Edinburgh Fringe Festival); *As You Like It, The Tempest, A Midsummer Night's Dream* (Blue Hutch Theatre Company) and for radio *The Hearing* and *Happy New Year* (Fuse FM).

Rebecca Lenkiewicz
The Painter

faber and faber

First published in 2011
by Faber and Faber Ltd
74–77 Great Russell Street
London WC1B 3DA

Typeset by Country Setting, Kingsdown, Kent CT14 8ES
Printed in England by CPI Bookmarque, Croydon, Surrey

A CIP record for this book
is available from the British Library

978-0-571-27673-8

2 4 6 8 10 9 7 5 3 1

Acknowledgements

Rebecca Lenkiewicz would like to thank Mehmet Ergen, Mel Kenyon, Leyla Nazli, Rachel Taylor, Ben Todd, Simon Trussler, Dinah Wood, all at the Arcola Theatre and the cast and company who made a huge contribution to the script

For my father, with love

Characters

Turner
thirties

William Turner
his father, sixties

Mary Marshall Turner
his mother, fifties

Jenny Cole
twenties

Sarah Danby
forties

Hereford
twenties

Man in Pub

The action takes place in Turner's studio
and around London from 1799 onwards.
It covers decades, but no attempt should
be made to 'age' Turner.

THE PAINTER

SCENE ONE

The studio. 1799. William Turner varnishes a medium-sized canvas of which we can only see the back. Turner walks in from the rain. He is a touch drunk. William nods. Turner comes and looks at the canvas that William has varnished. Turner nods. Then warms himself by the wood stove.

William What did they say?

Turner says nothing. William finishes the varnishing and puts a brush in turpentine.

Did they like it? Will they take it?

Turner nods. He looks at some sketches.

You been drinking? With that lot?

Turner does not reply.

Or by yourself?

Turner By myself.

William Town was mad again. The protests. Smashing up the machines. They were climbing up and over them with their hammers. Bonfires. It was almost a riot. I'll put your supper on.

William exits. There is a large canvas on the floor. Turner walks over and looks at it.

Turner I could paint better than them with both hands tied behind my back. I could paint better than them with my tongue.

*He feeds various papers into the wood stove and the
light changes. Purcell's 'Dido's Lament' sounds, but
slightly distorted. He pours himself a rum. Downs it in
one. Stares at the fire. He gets on the floor and looks at
the painting close up.*

SCENE TWO

*Sarah Danby's parlour. Sarah sews. She is heavily pregnant.
Turner moves a chaise longue for her. He sets it down.*

Sarah Thank you. That's perfect.

Turner Anything else?

Sarah No . . . I spoke to your mother yesterday. She told
me you got your Fellowship. That's wonderful. You
didn't say.

Turner Where are the girls?

Sarah They're in bed. Awake. They were outrageous
today. Screaming at each other. In the park.

Turner They miss John.

Sarah I keep thinking he'll walk through the door. Lu
talks about him. The others don't. But they know
something's happened. Mo's convinced that I might die
too. She won't let me out of her sight. She'll be out there
on the stairs in a minute. Sitting and watching me. My
sister wants us to move in with her.

Turner I thought you didn't get on.

Sarah It would be good for the girls. The countryside.
Did you never want to move out?

Turner No.

Sarah Have you found somewhere? For the gallery?

Turner Harley Street.

Sarah She's kicking. Come here, William. Feel.

Turner hesitates.

Does it scare you? . . . You might have to paint a woman with child one day.

Sarah places his hand on her stomach. He keeps it there reluctantly. And now takes it away.

Wasn't so bad, was it?

Sarah goes back to her sewing.

Your bag's in the kitchen. You always leave something behind. You should get yourself a young woman.

Turner Is there a shop for that, is there?

Sarah Will you celebrate the New Year?

Turner I saw an old man mudlarking yesterday. That'd be a nice way to see it in.

Sarah Really though? Suppose you could go anywhere? Where would you be?

Turner Rome. Paris. Amsterdam.

Sarah But if it wasn't about painting . . . ? If it was just about enjoying yourself?

Turner is slightly confused.

Just any place. No galleries.

Turner . . . Maybe Archangel . . . in the snow. You?

Sarah I'd be with John. And the girls. Would you go with somebody?

Turner No.

Sarah Did you never have a girl, William?

Turner What?

Turner stares at her.

Sarah Thank you. For visiting.

Turner You're not in hospital.

Sarah I am. Sort of.

Turner stares at her.

What are you thinking about? . . . Right now.

Turner The fundamental behaviour of water.

Sarah looks away. Turner starts to leave.

Sarah William. Don't come round again.
Or . . . for a while.
It's the smell. The turpentine. It makes me feel sick.

Turner takes this in, starts to leave.

Your coat. And book . . .

Turner does not go back for them.

Goodnight, William.

Turner leaves.

SCENE THREE

*Turner sits and looks through his notebooks. Noting
which studies he may develop. It is late. There is a
banging at his internal door. There are the sounds of a
woman crying and now the throwing of objects against a
wall. A bottle is smashed. William can be heard trying to
calm the woman. No distinct words are heard. Turner
listens to the sounds. He stops working for a moment.
Pours himself a rum. Then he resumes.*

SCENE FOUR

The next day. The studio. William stretches a canvas. He nails it to a frame and then leans the canvas up against several others. He takes some pigment and grinds it with a pestle and mortar. He pours some oil into a cup. He adds the oil to the pigment gradually. He packs a little pipe with tobacco. Turner enters with a cup of tea, practising Dutch.

Turner '*Heb je mijn baggage gezien?*' [*Phonetically, 'Hep yee mine bahhaze heezine?*']

 William looks at him.

Dutch. 'Have you seen my baggage?'

 Turner sees a fresh calling card on a table.

Who's this?

William A friend of Weston's. Asked about a portrait.

Turner Face painting?

William I told him that wasn't your line.

 Turner puts down his tea. He studies a drawing that is on a wooden board with a handle on it. He plunges it into a pail of water next to him. He applies some watercolour paint to certain areas of the picture. Now a different wash on a few other areas. And a third colour. He puts this board down to dry next to two others. He takes a second drawing on a board. He adjusts a detail or two with a pencil then plunges that one into the pail of water and colours it with three washes as he did the last one.

Ready for tomorrow are you?

Turner We'll leave here at one.

William You'll be an hour early. Weston's three-by-four is finished. He wants you to go for supper. See it hung up.

Turner No.

William It'll save on your mutton.

Turner Eight drawings we'll take.

William Give me a list and I'll find them.

Turner Nine just in case I got the timings wrong.

William I called on Dr Monro. Told him how things have been. He said it's only going to get worse. He described some of the treatments. They use water . . .

Turner keeps adding details. William moves towards the kitchen.

I'll put the supper on.

Turner I'm going out.

William Town'll be mad. Celebrating.

Turner Take some money. Get yourself a drink.

William No. I'll tidy up. And pack the pictures for tomorrow.

Turner puts his brush down and gathers his jacket and leaves. William starts to varnish a canvas. He lights some candles as the light fades. Varnishes some more. Then snuffs the candles and leaves the room. Dawn breaks.

SCENE FIVE

The studio. Dawn. Turner walks in. It is dark. He holds a candle. He is quite drunk but very controlled with it. Jenny walks in behind him. She is a touch drunk too but can handle herself. A woodstove glows.

14

Turner You know who the woman really was?

Jenny No. You've lost me.

Turner She's his mother. Venus. Naked. Turned back into her goddess self.

Jenny Someone kept your fire going for you. That's nice.

Turner She's toying with him. Torturing him like a cat would a bird.

Jenny Got a dram? Of gin or something? Where can I pee?

Turner Over there.

Jenny Ta.

Jenny walks behind a screen and pees while Turner pours some rum out from a bottle. He recites to Jenny.

Turner
'For Tyrian virgins bows and quivers bear
And purple buskins o'er their ankles wear.'

Jenny reappears and comes to collect her drink.

Jenny Poetry. Lovely. What next, then?

Jenny shivers a bit and comes to Turner and puts his arms on hers to warm her.

We'll go upstairs, will we?

Turner is awkward with this.

Turner I hope so.

Jenny You don't have to hope, do you? . . . You just moved in?

Turner reaches for his bottle and glasses.

Turner No.

Jenny Can I light some more candles?

15

She lights the candles.

They said you were famous in the pub?

Turner No.

Turner pours out two rums and drinks one.

Jenny Is this house yours?

Turner Yes.

Jenny All of it?

Turner Yes.

Jenny I might start painting if that's what you get for it.

Turner It's not all you get.

Turner pours himself another rum.

Jenny What else?

Turner Abuse. Ignorance. Clowns telling you what your work is about.

Turner gives Jenny a rum.

Look at these.

Turner picks up some bottles of pigment.

Fugitives. No one's using them. Too scared they'll fade.

Jenny So why have you got them?

Turner I'll use them. The others won't. They'll wait. How could you not, though? Look at them . . .

Turner looks at the colours. Jenny looks at his paintings.

Jenny How come you asked me back? I thought your models gave it out for free ?

Turner I paint trees.

16

Jenny laughs.

Jenny I bet some of the girls would still come over.

Turner They do. They line up. All round the building. Every morning. Only Fridays they have a day off.

Jenny Really, though? Will girls do it with you just because you're you?

Turner I tell you, Jane –

Jenny Jenny.

Turner I tell you, Jenny, I open my window at dawn. I look out. Just to see what's the weather like . . . I look up at the sky and then I look down . . . and they're all there. Staring up at me. Hopeful. Some wear their best clothes and others they just stand there naked, even in the winter. It's . . . heartbreaking.

Turner pours himself another rum.

Four days after I was born there were three suns in the sky. It was a phenomenon. What do you think that means?

Jenny Fuck knows.

Turner I've got a good feeling about this year. Good momentum.

Jenny They're full of promises. Abolish this. Reform that. But they never do. What about the dead? No fishing them back from the sea, is there?

Turner What? Who?

Jenny Those blacks . . . The captain threw all the sick ones overboard. In the middle of the ocean. And there were sharks everywhere. Fuck it. Let's go upstairs.

Turner says and does nothing.

I've had a lot of artists. Painters are the quietest.

Turner Really?

Jenny It's nice. Writers . . . that's a bit more like you're on the farm.

She rolls a cigarette and lights it. Turner enjoys watching her. She offers him a puff but he declines it.

I went round to model for a sculptor once. He was there in his dressing gown. Asked to see me naked. Then he started touching me all over. Slowly. He's stood behind me at one point cupping my buttocks one in each hand as if they were a fire. 'Cold?' I said. 'It is June.'

Turner What did he say?

Jenny 'I have to acquaint myself with your body in the first case. See if it'll respond. It's a very personal art.' He's breathing very hard. So I fuck off. Shall we . . . ? I need to get back in a bit. To my boy.

Turner How old is he?

Turner sits down by the woodstove. He opens the woodstove and throws a stick in. It blazes up. He takes some pages from a book and puts them in the fire. They make a different light. He watches them. Turner lies down on a cushion on the floor and keeps looking at the flames. Jenny sits near him.

Jenny Four.

Turner Why did you call him Noah?

Jenny I was in Dorset and my waters broke. On the beach. They shifted me to the boarding house. I wish I'd just laid down on the pebbles for a few hours and pushed. After he was born it rained. For days. Weeks. So I called him Noah. For the sea.

Turner looks at her face properly for the first time.

What?

Turner just keeps looking.

Upstairs.
    It's extra for talking.

Turner How much?

Jenny I'm joking. You're new to this, aren't you?
    I could take my clothes off. You could draw me.

Turner shakes his head.

What do you like to paint best?

Turner Chaos.

Jenny Why? . . . How do you paint chaos?

Turner looks at her, smiles, shrugs his shoulders.

Do you know any of the fashionables? Have you painted
them?

Turner They just want to know if a painting's hot.
Whether it'll gain. They've got one or two facts. And they
string them out like they were classicists.

Jenny We should do what the French did.

Turner Some of them are real. I made a couple of friends.

Jenny Fuck 'em. Even the friends. If they were friends
they'd give you their castle. So you wouldn't have to ask
anyone for anything.

Turner I don't ask. They ask me. They come to me.

*Turner raises his hand and stays with it in the air,
defiant, pissed. Jenny takes his hand down. She puts
his hand on her breast. He takes it away. He gets up
and walks round.*
    *Jenny gets up and pours herself another drink. She
approaches Turner and holds him. The door opens.
William looks around the door.*

William . . . It's all done. Drying now.

William leaves. Jenny waits for perhaps an explanation.

Turner I think we'd best not.

Jenny You're not getting your money back.

Turner Here's something for your boy.

Turner picks up a small piece of paper with sketches on it.

Jenny It's a dragon.

Turner Does he like the water? Your lad?

Jenny Loves it. Can't keep him away from the boats and the river.
Come and find me. I'm always in The Flag. And if I'm not, just wait a bit. I'm never out and about for long. Night.

Jenny gives Turner a kiss on the cheek and takes the picture. Turner sits and looks at a few pictures around him. William opens the door.

William Shall I lock up?

Turner Yes.

William She was . . . exotic. Goodnight.

Turner What's happening upstairs?

William She's asleep.

William leaves. Turner pours himself another rum and downs it in one. He sits back and really looks at one of the canvases. We do not see it. We just see his face. Taking it in, expressionless but intent. Studying.

SCENE SIX

The Academy. Turner stands at a lectern. William is behind him with a bundle of drawings in a portfolio. Turner addresses his students. He is terribly nervous and hungover, but trying to contain it. He has notes to read but decides to start informally. Extempore.

Turner Gentlemen I see some . . .

He looks around the invisible table, gathers himself. A pause.

New faces . . . Well, do any of you . . . Roman history . . . Is that window . . . ? Can you close it?

Pause.

There is no doubt, at least I hope not, that you are acquainted . . . not unacquainted . . . with . . .

Pause. Turner picks up a card with notes written on it.

Perspective. Gentlemen.

He reads.

'For the further advancement of the profession . . . Looking forward with the hope that ultimately the joint endeavours of concording abilities will . . .'

He abandons the notes. And leans around and with William's aid finds a picture. He holds it up. It is of three glass balls.

Three glass globes. With their varying reflections.

Turner leans round again and spends some time with William finding a different picture.

So. Another picture. A topographical view. Topography has reached its height in this country. There is a finite height for it to reach unfortunately.

Turner leans around and finds a study of a country view.

Copying will help you with the language of perspective. But not with true interpretation. You will find no better teachers than your own eyes, if you use them correctly, to see things as they are. Excuse me. I shall resume presently.

Turner walks away.

SCENE SEVEN

The studio. The same evening. Turner sits across from his mother. She stares at the floor. Then looks around.

Mary How was it? With the men?
  They were coming to buy.

Turner It went well.

Mary You're surprised.
  You didn't think I'd remember . . .

  Turner does not reply.

When I'm clear I'm lucid.

Turner Absolutely. I know that.

Mary Don't.

Turner What?

Mary Your tone. It was patronising . . . How's your copying?

Turner I haven't copied for years.

Mary See. We're talking, aren't we?

  Turner nods.

Nobody's rattling pans or spitting. There are some important collectors coming round. Next week.

Turner That's right. Fawkes recommended them.

Mary He recommended you, not them. You're the one he's helping.

Turner It works both ways.

Mary I know. About your decision.

Turner is wrong-footed.

Turner Which decision?

Mary I thought I was somewhere else just now. So you've decided.

Turner Decided what?

Mary Why do you want me put away?

Turner I don't, Ma.

Mary Why do you insist on calling me that? I'd prefer it if you didn't. Monro's your patron. You asked him his opinion about me. How could you do that?

Turner He's a doctor.

Mary You've betrayed me . . . You've consulted Monro. And told him I was mad.

Turner I didn't say that.

Mary Are you sending me to Bedlam?

Turner No. Monro said St Luke's would be good for you.

Mary Pa visited the lunatics. He paid his entrance fee. He liked the spectacle of it. He said it stank. And a woman gave birth on a floor covered in shit. Is that where you want me?

Turner St Luke's is clean. Reputable.

Mary Like you? You're selling me to the Indians. Filial. You never felt that did you? I never wanted your father. Or you.

Turner I'll make you some tea.

Mary You sound like one of your fashionables. All they can feel is fear. And it's rubbing off on you. They smother their embarrassment and terror with all their gabble.

Turner You keep cutting yourself.

Mary I'm making marks not cutting. It's protection. It moves the pain away from my head. Shame you feel. So did he. You've had advantages, though.

Turner Advantages?

Mary I never hurt you when you were a child. I never would have hurt you. I didn't, did I? They say you're worth a fortune. All because you can copy things.

Turner does not reply, despondent. Mary reaches out her hand to him. Turner moves slowly to take her hand. As he touches hers Mary takes her hand slowly from his. Shakes her head.

You remind me of a dog. At people's feet. Waiting to be liked. Stroked.

Turner moves away from her.

I thought I was at the farm. Your heart's a hole, Billy. At least I can feel. Even if it's only pain. You can love some waterfall but you can't feel anything for your own mother. If they were letting my blood you'd only want to get in the room to paint it.

Turner nods, sighs, Mary stares away from him.

Take my hand. I'm sorry. Love's all that matters. To love and to forgive. It's not about who's right. But who's in the most pain.

Turner takes his mother's hand.

When are they coming for me?

Turner Monro needs to visit.

Mary You're selling me like a black. For being different.
You're nothing to me now, Billy. Don't cry. Don't be sad.
Because there is nothing. Between us. Get your pencils.
Go and do your copying.

Turner does not move.

SCENE EIGHT

*A pub. William sits and drinks, across from a Man, who
is drinking too. William has had a few beers.*

William They killed it. With the taxes.

Man Your shop?

William Wigs. A full one, that's really something. You've
got your needle. That's like a fishing hook. You take a
couple of strands of hair. And knot them in. And you just
keep doing that . . . maybe thirty to forty thousand times.
Working both hands all the time to keep the tension.

William drinks.

I took up cutting instead. It paid the rent. But in the end
it's a lot of dead hair round your feet. Whereas a wig,
it's . . . it's . . .

*William raises his glass to the Man who toasts with
him.*

Man A wig.
Make money with it, did you?

William It was a living. There's a new bloke in the
market. Swallowing snakes he is. I asked him if it hurt.

' he says. 'You just pinch their tail and they'll hop in there. They can get through tiny holes. Smaller than you think.' It makes itself into a ball. Down his throat. Then he pulls it back. That's when it hurts. He used to gag. But now he's got used to it.

Man Did he have much of a crowd?

William No.

Man Did you give him anything?

William I gave him a bit. Sleeping rough, he is. Him and his snakes. My wife was the most beautiful woman you ever saw in your life. Touch something she would and people would want to give it to her whatever it was. Like she was some Hindu goddess. With a shrine. She'd brush past a piece of furniture with her hand. Pale. Long fingers. And whoever's it was, they'd say, 'Take it. You like it? Take it.'

Man How does he live with that? A snake? In and out of his throat.

William Same again?

William gets up from the table.

SCENE NINE

The studio. Turner studies a book of lithographs. A knock on the door.

Turner Come in.

Jenny walks in.

Jenny Sorry I'm late. I've been running around . . . These pictures of me. Who are they for?

Turner No one.

Jenny Can I have a drink?

Turner It's there.

Jenny pours herself a gin.

Jenny Will you have one?

Turner No.

Jenny starts to prepare the space for her pose, cushions, a sheet.

Jenny Why don't you use corpses?

Turner No. There's no breath. No movement.

Jenny You paint trees. They don't move.

Turner Course they do. They're always moving.

Jenny Are you doing men like this too?

Turner No.

Jenny Not interested?

Turner Too ugly.

Jenny laughs and pours another gin from the bottle.

Jenny Noah did some drawings for you with that paper you sent. Fuck, I meant to bring them.

Turner prepares his paper to sketch again. Jenny downs her gin in one.

We waved goodbye to you. From the cliff. But you didn't see. You were down on the dock. Staring at the sun. For ages. Doesn't that hurt your eyes?

Turner Same as you staring at a candle.

Jenny He had a great day. Thanks. He's still talking about it. How come you paint the sea such a lot?

Turner It's the light. And what's underneath. Terrifying. Can you swim?

Jenny No. I don't like it.

Turner I'll take you and Noah down to Margate. Teach you how.

Jenny Will you show us where you lived?

Turner Nothing to see.

Jenny Why did they send you there?

Turner My mother was ill. Shall we make a start?

Jenny I can't imagine you swimming.

Turner It's the only time I don't feel short. If I wasn't a painter I'd be a sailor.

Jenny smiles.

Jenny Seriously? If I wasn't a prozzy I'd be . . . Happy. I should stop really. I did try other stuff. Pins. Fuck pins. Then slop work. Shirts. Buttons.

Turner Don't move your top half for a minute.

Jenny I could get by on it. But not when it became the two of us . . . I did look for other work. But there was nothing. It was winter. Noah's legs one night – they went blue. I rubbed brandy all over him. I was terrified. I ran down to the workhouse with him in my arms. I'd always sworn I'd never go there . . . and the fuckers, they wouldn't let me in. Not without an order. So I did it.

Turner We'll do an hour. Three different poses.

Jenny pours herself one more drink.

Jenny The first time was horrible. I was terrified. I pretended I'd been at it for ages. Stupid. I could have made more if I'd said I was new. You know what they do to the young girls? To make the men think it's her first time . . . ?

They put leeches up her. So when he's inside her he doesn't notice she's ripped already. But he gets a sting and he thinks that's it. If the girl's funny about leeches they'll –

Turner Don't . . .

Jenny They'll put a few tiny bits of broken glass up her. Just enough to make a bit of blood flow . . . Me, I don't mind what happens. I'm old. But with them. It's not right. They're very young.

Turner pours himself a rum and downs it in one.

I was picked up for it just the once. A constable. He took me outside and questioned me.

Turner What happened?

Jenny He asked me how long I'd been whoring. He was quite excited. And drunk. I made myself cry. 'I'm so sorry,' I said. 'You're right. I did give in to his copious solicitations.' I thought he'd fine me. Or ask for one. That's what most of them do. I was hoping it'd be against the wall because he was huge. He'd be pretty heavy on top. But he just went a bit red and let me go. Mags, though. Last year. She was shipped off to Sydney. Australia.

Turner For whoring?

Jenny And running a disorderly house. It wasn't so much that. Someone had lost their watch. They don't give a fuck about girls and broken glass but as soon as it's about property they're down on you like anything. Probably she did steal it. But still. Fuck. For a pocket watch. 'A Noted Virago', the papers called her.

She was tough. Fierce. If your man hit her she hit him back. Have you been in fights?

29

Turner No. Not with a man. Lower body now.

Jenny lies back down on the floor and now pulls her skirts up and her legs further apart so that Turner can see her nakedness although we do not. He stands and prepares to sketch.

Jenny Like that?

Turner and Jenny take a few moments to get over the strangeness of the situation.

Are you comfortable up there, are you? Mr Turner?

Turner 'He who would search for pearls must dive below.'

Jenny Will you take yourself off upstairs after I've gone?

Turner cannot reply.

Turner Hermaphrodites.

Jenny What?

Turner Half man, half woman. The Greeks believed we were all both sexes in one body originally. Then we were cut in two. And the rest of our lives is a search for that lost half.

Jenny So half of me is a man somewhere? And half of you is a woman?

Turner If she looks like me I don't want to find her.

Jenny smiles. Turner settles down now and sketches. A knock on the door. Turner does not leave his drawing and shouts through.

No!

Another knock.

Not in. Working.

The door opens and Sarah walks in, but Turner does not look round to see her.

Leave it outside the door.

Sarah I'm sorry. But I was troubled.

Turner looks around.

Turner Sarah . . .

Sarah You're working. I'll only be a moment.

Sarah walks towards Turner.

I'm sorry. About the other evening.

Turner It's not the best time.

Sarah I only want a minute.

Sarah sees Jenny now. Tries not to be too wrong-footed.

Oh. I see. I'm . . . interrupting. You should have said. You're . . . involved.

Jenny sits up, pulls her clothes around her.

Turner It's –

Sarah I'm sorry. Excuse me. I didn't realise you –

Turner It's anatomy.

Sarah Yes.

Turner The female form.

Sarah Yes. I see that.

She leaves. Turner puts down his drawing board. Breathes. Jenny stands up.

Jenny Who was that?

Turner A neighbour.

Jenny Married?

Turner Her husband just died.

Jenny Everyone loves widows.
    She likes you.
    She's nice looking. Tight, though. Her face. She wants
you.

Jenny sees something of the sketch.

Strange looking, aren't we? Does it come out exactly as
you want it to?

Turner No. That's the work of it.

Jenny When you're looking at things, do you just see
them as pictures?

Turner I'm waiting a lot of the time. Sifting stuff.

Jenny What would you do? If you couldn't see?

Turner I'd kill myself, no question. You?

Jenny I couldn't. Not with Noah.

*Jenny closes her eyes. She feels her own face a little.
Then Turner's arm and his face. Then she opens them.*

Billy, I saw a man. On London Bridge. Did I tell you?
No. It was Thursday. He was shouting. Pissed. Swaying.
He had no shoes. He'd taken his shirt off and he was
saying he'd jump. He was being so loud about it and I
thought he was just looking for attention. I walked past
on the other side. And I swear he seemed to be staring at
me. He went quiet then. And he just stepped off . . . as
though there was a platform. In the air. I felt sick, Billy.
Like I'd be sick.

Jenny becomes melancholic. She weeps.

Sorry, Billy. It's just the gin. But it is the fucking loneliest
city in the world, London. Isn't it?

Jenny lies down again. She starts to really cry now,
weepy with the drink. Turner keeps drawing her.

SCENE TEN

The Academy. Turner lectures to his students. He is still
nervous, but has abandoned the formal cards. He has a
large notebook he can refer to.

Turner If you'd like to sit if you're going to stay . . . And
could you close that door . . .?

The sublime. A dark event. A maelstrom. It can have
its own beauty. The captain of a slave ship. Collingwood.
He is told that he will receive insurance for any blacks
who are lost at sea. But not for those who are dead on
arrival. He does not want to lose money, so he inspects
the hulls. He gathers up those slaves who are sick and
might not last the journey. He marches them up on to
the deck. In the middle of the night. The sea is black.
And shark infested. He has his men remove the slaves'
shackles. And then throws them overboard. They scream.
Struggle. Cry out for some minutes. And then they are
simply the sound of the sea. He suspects his crime is
hidden in the vastness of that ocean. Under cover of night.
A sailor recounts it. It is up to us to paint it. Record it.
Put that man on trial for the rest of history. Forget about
dogs. Face-painting. Flowers. There is sometimes a duty.
To record. And to paint such violence but with a beauty –
that would be something. We'll resume. Presently.

Turner leaves.

*The studio. William hauls in long herring nets. Two
stepladders are at either side of the walls. Turner comes
in and together they hang the nets high up and flat near
the ceiling. Then Turner lays tissue paper on the nets. He
steps down and looks at a picture on the wall. William
observes Turner and the picture. Turner looks up at the
light as it diffuses through the tissue. Bright sunshine
streams through.*

William How is it?

*Turner nods. Watches the painting again. He climbs up
a ladder to adjust the tissue. Comes down. Looks.
Nods.*

Yes?

Turner It'll have to be bigger. Everything'll be scaled up
by maybe twenty.

William But it works in principle?

Turner The light's good. It's diffusing.

William More nets, then.

A door closes in the next room to theirs.

Turner We'll get them sewn together into one, else
there'll be seams. Lines in the light. It's got to be perfect.
And we'll paint the walls red.

William Red?

Turner Carmine. And vermilion.

William Red.

Turner They laugh at me.

William Who?

34

Turner At the Academy. They think I'm out of my depth. The wrong class.

William No.

Turner They do. But no matter.

William I looked at their work.

Turner What did you think?

William Nice lines. No ideas.

Turner Who's next door?

William looks through a spy-hole in the wall.

William It's the widow.

Turner looks through the spy-hole.

Turner Can you tell her I'm not in?

William No.

Turner does not answer. Turner starts to line some wood up for stretchers. William leaves. Turner starts to make a frame to stretch a canvas on. He measures the wood.

A gentle knock. Sarah walks in and watches him. She is behind him. She starts to walk towards him and he hears her and looks at her. He is on his knees. He gets up.

Turner Hello.

Turner puts his tools down.

How are you?

Sarah I've brought your books.

Turner and Sarah look at each other. He measures up another piece of wood.

Turner I'm sorry. If you felt . . . awkward . . . the other night.

Sarah I blushed. That was all.

Pause. Turner shows Sarah a red pigment.

Turner What do you think of this? For the gallery?

Sarah It looks like Napoleon's bedroom.

Turner He's got a David he hangs in his bathroom. Philistine. He was teased. About his accent. He couldn't spell.

Sarah Do you admire him?

Turner He's a butcher. But his numbers are impressive.

Turner looks at the books that Sarah has returned, awkward.

Sarah It wasn't that girl's nudity that made me blush. I've seen enough of that backstage. It was her being so near to you.

Turner She's a model.

Sarah And a prostitute.

Turner She tried other stuff.

Sarah You defend her.

Turner What?

Sarah We keep doing this. Missing each other's mark.

Turner takes a knife and starts to cut some wood.

Be careful . . . of your hands.

Sarah picks up a sketch.

You work too hard.

Turner Rubens produced three thousand paintings. Harley Street's got to be the biggest. The best.

Sarah Why?

Turner It's going to be epic. We can fit a hundred people in there.

Sarah But you produce work for yourself, don't you?

Turner It's by me. Not for me. You didn't act for yourself, did you?

Sarah It's sad that money ever has to come into the equation.

Turner Is it? Velazquez always wanted a knighthood. He petitioned everyone. Even the Pope. He had to write a letter apologising for ever having asked for money for his work. Because a gentleman would never do that. They kept refusing him.

Sarah Did he ever get it?

Turner A year before he died . . . People think that the act of putting paint on canvas, that should be enough of a reward. But it's a dance . . . Velazquez! Writing a letter. Of apology.

Sarah Would you like a knighthood? Would that settle you?

Turner I'm not ill.

Sarah But you chase.

Turner No. I work. I record. That's what I do.

Sarah I've offended you.

Turner They'd never have me in their stable anyway. Constable, maybe. Not me. A rough at court? No. 'Mr Turner, alas, feels the perpetual need to be extraordinary.' Why would you want to be anything else?

Sarah You shouldn't read reviews.

Turner A friend quoted it to me . . . You're extraordinary. When you act.

Sarah I won't be able to go back to it. I'm sorry – that our friendship has gone awry.

Turner Has it?

Sarah Who's the best out of Rubens and Velazquez?

Turner Velazquez almost puts your eyes out he's so good. And Titian. And Claude. Fuseli. France I need to get to. Italy. What's here is mostly useless. English painting is dead. It's dealers making fortunes out of sentimental dross. Dogs. Cherubs.

Sarah sees a circle wheel of colour on paper with tones from dark to light on it.

Sarah What's this?

Turner It's the tonal scale. From Rooker. Watercolours they're transparent. So you work from light to dark. I'll work on maybe four at the same time. Do the first tone on all of them. Then the second.

Sarah looks at an open sketchbook.

Sarah And these are of where?

Turner Yorkshire. It rained so much I was webfoot.

Sarah Webfoot?

Turner I was. Like a drake.

Sarah You're different in here.
You're freer.

Turner looks at Sarah. She smiles. They look at each other properly for the first time.

William.

Turner Yes?

Sarah Why were you angry when I talked about your love life?

Turner I haven't got a love life. So you couldn't be talking about it. Could you? I wasn't. Angry.

Turner kneels down to sort the stretchers.

Sarah Why haven't you got one?

Turner If I went out somewhere I'd want to take my sketchbook with me. And girls don't like the smell of paint.

Sarah I didn't mean it when I said that.

Sarah stands into him so that her skirt is next to him. He ignores the touch of the material. Sarah goes to her knees and kisses him. Turner kisses her strongly. Then stops.

Turner Sorry.

Sarah Why? Lie next to me.

Turner I've thought about that.

Sarah Have you?

Turner A lot.

Sarah You should have said.

Turner I didn't imagine . . .

Sarah That I wanted that? I do.

Sarah kisses Turner. They become very passionate. Turner breaks away.

Turner Sorry.

Sarah You need to think less.

Let your guard down. Trip up. Fall down. Between my legs.

Turner Am I allowed to think about that?

Sarah You are.

He kisses her again. Then stops. Takes her face in his hands and looks at her intently.

Turner Come upstairs. Please.

Sarah Don't say please.

Turner Come upstairs.

Sarah Yes.

Turner Thank you.

Turner realises he should not have thanked Sarah. He walks towards the door in front of her, then opens it for her.

SCENE TWELVE

Six months later. The studio. Mary sits. William stands, waiting for Turner. There is a travelling bag next to her.

Mary He carries on with her but he won't marry?

William I'll take your bag for you.

Mary Leave it. Months he's been going to hers after dark. Like some sort of animal.

Turner enters with Sarah.

Turner Monro's outside. He's waiting for the coach.

Mary The baby's not yours. The widow's child.

Sarah Mary . . . how are you?

Mary Your musician. His hands changed. They became like hooks.

Sarah They did. He died.

Mary He couldn't play any more. But they're not locking him up. Another child you have.

Sarah Yes. John's baby.

Mary But you two . . . carry on.

Turner does not reply.

Sarah William has helped me. A great deal.

Mary He's not helped me. You've been kind, Sarah. These two weren't. At least your John died at home. With windows. I have been through such violence. In my head.

Sarah Perhaps . . . at the hospital . . .

Turner Monro says the doctors there are the best.

Mary He says a lot. I shan't need my clothes.

Sarah You will. Of course you will.

Mary No I won't. They're worried that I might kill myself in my bedroom. But I think it would be kinder to let me hang from a rafter here than fester there.

Sarah The treatments . . . they might alleviate the pain. And then you can come home.

Mary They won't have me here, Sarah. They just won't.

She takes some clothes out of her bag.

Sarah Mary . . .

Mary I shan't need them.

Sarah Let's put them back. They'll hang them up for you there.

Mary I'm not a child. I know what they do. They keep you naked there. I want nothing from here. I shall have to stop talking soon. We'll all stop talking. And then it will be time.

William I'll see if the coach is here.

Mary Don't. They'll come in. Am I keeping you from something? More important?

Turner Ma . . . don't.

Mary Don't what? What am I not to do now? Sarah, don't trust these men. They're cold. And they'll try to kill you. They will.

Mary hangs her underwear over Turner's canvases.

So. I take my leave of you. Come and draw me in there. Dead. You wouldn't save me if I was drowning, would you, Billy? Your money. It's nothing. It's filthy. You're all on the inside. Since it happened to me they're all trying to get in. I need someone from the outside. To hear me. Someone who's not biased. Prejudice is a terrible thing. They all want to violate me. As if I was a girl again. The men from the market came here this morning. Lining up for me. Shouting. They want to lock me in a shed somewhere and use me there. Like a heifer. And you don't stop them, Billy. You say 'Ma this' and 'Ma that' but you just stand there and do nothing.

A man waits outside for Mary. William gathers her clothes in her case. Turner exits. Sarah follows him. William guides Mary gently by the shoulders.

Who are you? Running around after him. Like a lackey. I hate you.

William nods.

I hate you.
    I hate you. Help me.

William holds Mary. They hold each other. Then William attempts to lead her out of the room. Turner appears at the door with Sarah.

I need to say goodbye. To Billy. Alone.

Turner walks in. William walks out. Sarah starts to walk away.

Turner Sarah. Stay.

Sarah Your mother wants to say goodbye to you.

Turner Please. Stay.

Sarah stands near the door, half there, half not. Mary puts her hand out to Turner. He walks to her and takes it.

Mary When you were a boy I would take you down to the docks. And sometimes when the ebb tide was at flood the river was so high that the boats would shoot over London Bridge – do you remember that?

Turner nods.

I bought you a paint box. For Christmas. In a wooden case. You were ten. I put it by your bed. In the dark. And you woke. And your hands shook when you were opening it. I had to help you because you were so excited.

Turner You'd drawn on the paper.

Mary I only prayed the once. Truly prayed. When your sister was dying. The Christmas after that one. Mary. She was eight. Do you remember?

Turner Yes.

Mary I knelt on the ground. I looked at her face. Fevered. In pain. And I looked at you stood by the door. Watching us all. And I prayed. I said, 'God, please, if you could just take one of my children, then take Billy. Let Mary live.'

You weren't even ill but I said, 'Billy can die, God. But please let me keep my daughter.'

Turner takes his hand away from his mother.

What? She was beautiful, wasn't she? Your sister? She was an angel.

Mary walks out. Turner stands there and Sarah joins him now. And they hold each other.

SCENE THIRTEEN

The Academy. Turner lectures to his students.

For composition. Respect your paper. Keep your corners quiet. Centre your interest.

Mechanical rules. You may be a genius, but you must first learn your craft. Rules are not fetters. They only limit those with no talent. For those who are strong they are a defence. For those who are weak and confused rules are indeed shackles.

You, sir, you seem to be enjoying a conversation in the back there . . . You drew a dog last week, didn't you? A dog with an open mouth. And legs that would not support a chicken. We will resume. Imminently.

SCENE FOURTEEN

The studio. Jenny wanders round, looking at drawings. She goes to a mirror and looks at her face. She finds some water in a basin and cleans off some of her rouge. Turner walks in.

Turner Jenny. You're early.

Jenny On time. That's a first, isn't it?

Turner You look different.

Jenny How's your week been? Mine's been mayhem. Thank God for Kent. If we didn't go there I'd go mad, I really would. Noah sent you some pictures.

Jenny gives a roll of a few pictures to Turner. He does not undo them.

Turner Thank him for me.

Jenny You'll see him. At the weekend. Are you not going to have a look? He did a crocodile. And a pirate ship. He used that triangle thing you showed him . . . What is it?

Turner Why?

Jenny You always look at them.

Turner I will. Later.

Jenny Is something wrong?

Turner No. Nothing's wrong. I . . .

Jenny Has something happened?

Turner No. Yes.

Jenny Are you chucking me out?

Turner What?

Jenny She's told you to clear out your studio. Have a good clean. Get rid of all the filth.

Turner No . . .

Jenny Oh. Good. What then?

Turner Yes. She has.

Jenny I thought so. I'm surprised she left it this long. She's got a point. I wouldn't want my fella staring into some other woman's cunt. No matter.

Turner I've got some money for you. Because there was no notice.

Jenny Keep it . . . Spend it on Noah. It's a shame. It was very . . . peaceful. Are we doing today's session?

Turner No.

Jenny So . . . I've an hour to do exactly what I please. I'll just put something warmer on.

Jenny takes some woollen garments from her bag. She stands away from Turner and takes off her shirt so that her back is to him and naked. He is aware of her.

It's nice. Being painted. You sit back and go places. Last week I closed my eyes and I kept seeing all those orchards we passed. And those rows and rows of hops. Everything slows down. I'll miss the smell. Maybe I'll take some jars. To remind me.

Jenny, dressed now, goes to Turner and shakes his hand.

Thanks. It's been great. So I'll see you on Saturday. At the station. Same time as usual.

Turner looks awkward.

Won't I?

Turner I can't.

Jenny What?

Turner She wants me to stop seeing you. Altogether.

Jenny But he's a child. He won't understand. She's a . . . We've never touched each other. Not once.

Turner Sarah asked if I was his dad.

Jenny He's four years old. What is she, a fucking halfwit?

46

Turner She thinks I'm lying about it.

Jenny Suspicious fucking bitch. What do you talk about with her?

Turner What?

Jenny Does she make you laugh? No.

Turner What?

Jenny You're worth more than that. Why did you agree to it?

Turner She was upset.

Jenny I'm upset. All of London's upset. Every fucking day. Doesn't mean you can take it out on some innocent stranger.

Turner I'm sorry.

Jenny No, you're not. You never do a thing that you don't want to do. Do you love her?

Turner does not answer.

Do you love anyone?

Turner Take the money.

Jenny Keep your fucking blood money. She's trained you. Some people fall in love and some simply train each other up.

Turner Nobody's trained me.

Jenny You're her dog.

Turner I'm not her fucking dog –

Jenny She's got you jumping and you don't even know that you're doing it.

Turner She needs me. She's got four daughters.

Jenny You're a coward, Billy. You only met her because she lives next fucking door. You hide in here and you're terrified of anything approaching real life. No matter. We're all as bad as each other. I'll see you, then.

Jenny goes to Turner and they hold each other and she gives him a gentle kiss on the cheek. They don't want to let each other go. Turner kisses Jenny's neck. She kisses him back. They kiss. She stops kissing him now, but stays in his arms.

Jenny I'm not . . . I don't . . . I've been drinking gin all day.

Turner You don't taste of gin.

Jenny kisses him again. Then starts to leave, upset. She walks back towards him.

Jenny I told Noah you were his dad . . . I told him you were his father, but we couldn't all be together.

Turner What? Why would you say that?

Jenny When he was ill. He said he wished you were his dad. So I told him you were. But that it was a secret. You're the only man he's known, Billy. Who's been kind to him. He talks about you. He points to men who are fishing in the distance and asks if they're you. He waves at boats. Asks if you're on them. You taught him things.

Turner Children shouldn't be lied to. He won't thank you for it. When he's older.

Jenny I don't think he'll make it that far . . . You don't see him nights. And I don't give a fuck about the truth. Who's to say you weren't his dad for a few months?

Turner I'm not . . . his dad.

Jenny What's a father anyway?

Turner It's not me.

48

Jenny No. Maybe not . . . but I'd say anything to make him that bit happier. You don't know. You've not had a child. I worry about him . . . And I worry about you. That you'll never let yourself fall. Truly.

Turner I should get on now. Take that money. Really.

Jenny No. You can't even let me say goodbye. You're a beautiful hypocrite, Billy. You're scared and you don't even know it. You want to try just living for a change sometime. See how it feels.

Turner I do live . . . I do. Just . . . somewhere else.

Jenny walks out.

SCENE FIFTEEN

The Academy. Turner lectures.

Nature is wild. Cruel. Never be afraid to put your brightest light next to your deepest shadow on the centre. But not in the corners. You must mark the greater from the lesser truth. Express the larger idea, not the narrow and confined. Landscapes are seen as static. Rooted. They're not. Don't be a slave to what you see. It may rain. You don't have to paint it. Look past it. Select, combine and concentrate that which is beautiful. Hannibal . . . he chose to . . . no matter. We'll resume presently.

Turner leaves.

SCENE SIXTEEN

The studio. Turner notes something down in a book. Sarah knits.

Sarah What are you writing?

Turner Nothing.

  A beat.

Sarah Did you talk to . . . ?

Turner Yes.

Sarah How was she about it?

Turner Dignified.

Sarah Were you ever her . . . client?

Turner No.

Sarah Were you somebody else's?

Turner Why do you want to know?

Sarah Because I'm with you. I asked you to do something that meant a lot to me. I didn't demand it. Or dictate it.

Turner I asked you for something.

Sarah I don't want you to draw me like that.

Turner I didn't want to turn Jenny out.

Sarah You talk as though she were living with you.

Turner She was a friend. She was the closest I've ever had to a sister.

Sarah I hope that's not how your sister would have ended up.

Turner You were an actress.

Sarah That doesn't mean I was a whore. But she is. A whore. I'm not judging her. I'm stating what she is.

Turner She's got a boy to support. She's a good mother.

Sarah I've four daughters. It's what women do.

Turner He's a sweet boy.

Sarah You've met him?

Turner We took him down to see the ships. In Margate. He'd never seen the sea. He was fantastic. Racing the waves he was.

Sarah You don't take the girls out. With me. We live as though someone will cut our throats if we were ever to play happy families.

Turner I don't know that we're . . .

Sarah What?

Turner We started out well.

Sarah We're not a horserace . . . It's not been long. Give it time. We need to attune.

Turner Do we? Don't people simply . . . ?

Sarah No. They don't. It takes time. And practice.

Turner Training . . . Sarah . . .

Sarah Yes?
William . . .

Sarah takes his hand and puts it against her stomach. She puts his hand just above her pubis bone.

Can you feel that? How it's harder there? My stomach. It's my womb. That's us. There.

Turner You're . . . ?

Sarah Yes.
Kiss me. And keep your hand on my stomach.

They kiss.

Turner Do you love me?

Sarah You've to think less, William. Billy. Just trust. I'm here. We're here.

She kisses him.

Turner Will you leave? Or change? Towards me?

Sarah No.

Turner Never?

Sarah Never.

Turner When you acted, did it feel like lying?

Sarah No. Never.

Turner looks at Sarah's stomach. She kisses him lightly. Turner breathes, kisses her strongly.

SCENE SEVENTEEN

Six months later. Turner writes a list in his notebook. William enters, distracted. Hereford looks in at the door, visible to us but not to father and son.

Turner Take the day off if you want to.

William I don't. We're busy. There's a buyer waiting.

Turner I don't want to see anyone. Why don't these people give us some notice? It's not a fucking soup kitchen . . .

Hereford I'm here, Mr Turner. I'm sorry if I'm . . . but I have travelled. I didn't know there was a system in place.

Turner An appointment will do.

Hereford I'd like an hour if you can spare it.

Turner I can't.

Hereford I want to buy a few pieces. I'm quite serious.

Turner I'm serious too.

Hereford enters and William leaves.

Hereford Of course. Time is money.

Turner No. Time is time.

Hereford cannot reply.

You want something big or you want something small?

Hereford Monro said you had a dry sense of humour.

Hereford sees some dried-up paint brushes.

Are these pencils done for? In which case I'd buy them off you.

Turner I'm not dead . . . If you could be brief I would appreciate it.

Hereford I'm an admirer. A fan. It's fascinating for me. To see you in your own environment. You're the first in your department, Mr Turner, you really are.

Turner does not reply.

I own a bit of everyone. But nothing of yours yet. Weston said there was talk of Twickenham. And a floating studio?

Turner I might buy a boat.

Hereford Wonderful. Giles Hereford. Lloyds of London. I collect internationally. For my own viewing. Not for commercial use.

Turner There's a body of my work at the Academy at the moment. If you'd like to have a look. Here is anarchy. As you can see.

Hereford looks at a canvas.

Hereford These are very nice. Your arboreal forms.

Turner Trees.

Hereford Do you need more staff? I know people. It's probably a bit much for the old boy, isn't it?

Turner He starts the paintings and he finishes them.

Hereford laughs.

Hereford It's good to keep the ancient employed.

Turner You shouldn't talk of the old like that.
He's my father.

Hereford nods, awkward.

Hereford I paint. As well as collect. So I do understand. The process.

Turner What do you paint?

Hereford Anything. Everything.

Turner Then you're making a mistake before you even start. Do you sketch?

Hereford Regularly.

Turner How many times will you record a subject?

Hereford Once . . . generally.

Turner . . . What colour is your front door?

Hereford Black.

Turner Describe it to me.

Hereford It's black.

Turner Show me your hands.

Hereford takes off his gloves and shows Turner his clean hands.

You're not a painter.

Hereford Not everyone uses their fingers. Or spits on the canvas.

Turner Fuck off.

Hereford looks at Turner.

I just asked you to leave.

Hereford I heard you.

Pause.

So . . . I'll buy elsewhere.

Turner Good. Go on then. You've met your hero, now fuck off.

Hereford I'm sorry. That we couldn't talk. Properly.

Turner breathes heavily. He sits now. He puts his head between his hands. Hereford watches, fascinated. He is in no hurry to leave.

Mr Turner? Are you not well? Shall I get you something?

Turner does not move.

Some water?

William looks in through the door. He comes straight in to Turner and holds him tight.

William Billy. Billy? It's all right. Don't get yourself in a state about it.

Hereford He just seemed to . . .

William His mother. They moved her today. From hospital.

Hereford To where?

William To Bedlam.
It's all right, Billy.

Hereford still watches the famous man in his emotion.

William Fuck off, will you? My son's not well. Or can't you see that?

Hereford nods, leaves.

Billy.

William gives Turner a cup of water. Turner gets up and walks to the back of the studio. He goes behind the screen and is sick into a bucket, his back to his father.

That's all right. Best get it out.

Turner comes out, wipes himself with a rag.

You need to stop today. Rest.

Turner She said how her dad had paid to watch the inmates before. Like a circus.

William They don't do that now. No paying public.

Turner They're still in there, though, aren't they? They're just invisible.

Father and son sit, not touching, trying to take in the situation.

SCENE EIGHTEEN

The studio. Sarah walks around looking at the sketches. She is heavily pregnant now. She is looking for the series that depicts Jenny. She looks at a book. A newspaper clipping falls out. Sarah picks it up. Reads it. William walks in.

William Sarah.

Sarah Hello.

William Don't see you in here often.

Sarah He's saved this. 'Mr Turner, whose genius we so much admire, has been long trifling with his fame, and playing upon the borders of extravagance as if in pursuit of his attainment. We hope, now he has reached it, he may be induced to abandon these experiments.'

William Bastards. He's at the Academy.

Sarah I know. We'll all go later, will we?

William In your condition?

Sarah Of course. I was looking. For William's anatomical sketches. Of Jenny . . . How was the visit? To Mrs Turner.

William They'd cut all her hair off. Looked like they'd used a knife. Blood and . . . all over her head. They don't bother to clean them up very much. It's not very clever.

Sarah Does she know where she is?

William She fades in and out.

Sarah What did Monro say?

William That the descent will be fast. A few weeks, he said.

Sarah William refuses to go there.

William I can't force him.

Sarah I'm sorry. What was he like? As a boy?

William He'd always be looking up. Other children they'd be looking down. To find stuff. Anything. On the streets. He'd be staring up. At the sky.

Sarah And Mary was ill even then?

William It was always there. Less evident, though.

Sarah He said she couldn't stand to be in the same room as him.

William Cruel, she was. Said things a child should never hear. Did things he never should have seen. And when little Mary died she just lost it. She'd lock herself up. Disappear. I'd take him down to see the boats. Teach him to swim. And fish. He only wanted to please her. We both did.

Sarah He should see her, don't you think? For his own peace of mind.

William He's terrified he'll end up like her. He thinks it's in him. The madness.

Sarah He doesn't want me here any more. He hasn't said it. But I can feel it. I thought that our having a child might change things.

William I should put the meat on.

Sarah I do love him, William.

William starts to study a canvas.

As much as you can love somebody who's absent.

The outside door goes. William shouts.

William Billy? You're back early? How was it?

Turner walks in from the street, carrying a portfolio.

Turner It was . . . good. Sarah.

Sarah Hello.

Turner Hello.

Turner takes a breath. Calms down. He pours himself a rum.

58

I wish you'd been there, Dad. You should have come.
They were hysterical. Running around. No amount of
light is going to repair some of those monsters they've
created.

William Lots of rubbish?

Turner Most of it's woefully weak. There's a few
interesting ones.

William Any trouble?

Turner No. They put me in the best space. It looks
impressive.

William It'll sell then?

Turner I took it off the list. I'm not going to sell it.

William What do you mean?

Turner It's one of the family.

William You're joking me.

Turner No. We don't need the money.

William You're soft, Billy.

Turner Am I? No. No, it's a good decision

William walks out.

Sarah That's lovely. That you'll keep it.

Turner I'm tired of them all going away.

Sarah Are you looking forward to the child? Our child.

Turner I am.

Sarah Are you? You're always . . . somewhere else.

Turner No.

William walks in.

59

William I've put some stew on. We can eat early.

Sarah We could eat at Rule's on the way? We're celebrating, aren't we?

William and Turner share a look.

Turner You've made it now, haven't you?

William Chopped. Not cooked.

Turner Let's eat here. I can't face any more of all that today.

William How much would they have to offer to make you change your mind?

Turner No amount. I'd like to be buried in it if I'm honest.

William What?

Turner Have it as my winding sheet. In the earth.

William I'll get changed. Have a wash.

He exits.

Sarah You've money but you won't eat out.

Turner It's all the . . . service. And people doing things for you. And . . . wine. It takes too long.

Sarah John loved us to eat together. We'd talk. Have some time. Alone . . . I came down here to find the sketches you did. Of Jenny.

Turner They're not in here.

Sarah Did you give them to her?

Turner No.

Sarah Do you love me?

Turner What?

Sarah I've been waiting. For you to love me. I thought it would happen. But it hasn't.

Turner What do you mean? . . . We don't argue.

Sarah I dreamt that you were with Jenny. That I was sat in the corner of our bedroom watching the two of you. And you were lying with your head next to her feet. And you were touching them very gently. And you were kissing her ankles. And you were just so happy.

Turner It was a dream. A fiction.

Sarah But I feel ashamed. Apologetic. And that's not me. If you want me gone you should tell me.

Turner I don't.

Sarah I need more, William.

Turner I don't know how to give more.

Sarah And I don't know how to live with this little.

Turner I'll try. To improve.

Sarah No. It's not school. When the baby's born. If you still want to. You can draw me. Nude.

Turner You don't want me to.

Sarah I've changed my mind.

Turner You don't have to do that.

Sarah I want to.

Turner No.

Sarah I want to. Please.

Turner Why?

Sarah I want you to draw me. I want you to.

Sarah kisses Turner's cheek and leaves him alone.

SCENE NINETEEN

*The Academy. Turner lectures. William has pictures
behind him. Turner and William both wear black
mourning bands. William looks at the floor.*

Turner Painting is a curiously private activity. Private.
Then . . . public.

Silence.

You have to be strong enough. Agile. In your vision.
To handle the public side of it. But then not to allow that
to contaminate . . . your privacy. The independent artist.
He will prefer to be a beggar and do good work than
crawl to a patron and produce incompetent . . . scraps.
An idea for a painting. 'A Burial at Sea.' Two tall fighting
ships. And a tiny coffin between them. With the sun
catching the tiny wooden structure as it goes into the
waves. The vastness of nature versus the small scale of
man. In his box. Whilst live men are on two larger
floating boxes. A painting is the most beautiful escape
you could ever wish for.

Silence.

A picture.

*Turner looks round. William has not reacted. Turner
looks through the drawings. William looks at the
students and at Turner. William sits down on the floor,
puts his head in his hands. And weeps. Turner sees
this. Then looks round at the students.*

Laughing, are you? Laughing? I'll take you. Outside. Now.

He gathers himself.

Go back to your work. Go.

He looks at his students.

SCENE TWENTY

The studio. Turner sits opposite Jenny. She is pale.

Jenny Sorry.

Turner Don't keep apologising.

Jenny I just wanted to tell you. I'll go in a minute.

Turner Stay as long as you like. Dad can make a bed up for you.

Jenny No. Not many people knew him really. Apart from the other girls. And you.

Turner I wish you'd told me before.

Jenny Haven't been able to move. I just lay down for a week. Since I got up I've not really been thinking very straight.

Turner What can I do? To help?

Jenny Nothing. Everything's slower. Like I took opium. Wish I had.

Turner Are you in the same place?

Jenny I'll move. I can't stay there. Not now. It's full of him, you know?

Turner Can I do anything?

Jenny No one can. It's very strange. Like I can only think one thought at a time. It's like I've taken something. Thanks, though. Shall I come again?
  I need to do a few things. Or I'll just stop.

Turner Take some money.

Jenny No. I'd only get high on it. I might wake up and think he was still here.

Turner Please. Take it.

Jenny No. I don't need it for anything. He was beautiful, wasn't he?

Turner He was. And sharp. And his imagination –

Jenny He was kind too. If anyone was . . . he worried . . . about the children. He saw a family sleeping on the streets. He said we could put them in our bed with us. Do you have his drawings? I'd like them.

Turner has thrown them out.

Turner I'll look for them . . . after you've gone. The place is a mess.

Jenny You haven't got them, have you?

Turner Somewhere. Just . . . you know what it's like in here.

Jenny Don't worry. It's only bits of paper. It's not really him, is it?

Jenny cries. Turner cannot comfort her.

Will you walk me to the corner?

Turner takes a moment to reply.

Actually, don't.

She looks at Turner's model ships which are on a shelf in a glass casement.

He was crazy about those ships. He asked you for them, didn't he? You said they weren't a toy.

Turner I'm sorry.

Jenny No. You're right. They're not. But I don't think he wanted to play with them. He just wanted to put them in his corner. And look at them. Goodnight.

Jenny shakes his hand. And leaves.

SCENE TWENTY-ONE

The Academy. Turner lectures.

Turner We must aim as high in painting as the most exalted poets. Investigate the universal truths of our existence. 'And I saw an angel standing in the sun . . . and he cried with a loud voice . . . saying to all the fowls that fly in the midst of heaven, "Come and gather yourselves together unto the supper of the great God; that ye may eat the flesh of kings, and the flesh of captains and the flesh of mighty men, and the flesh of horses, and of them that sit on them, both small and great."'
  Bathe in the past. Then forget it. Explode it.

Turner has slightly wandered. He comes back to his students.

Hannibal. He was told it was impossible to cross the Alps. Impossible. But he didn't listen . . . Rather like you, sir. Not listening.

Turner walks away.

SCENE TWENTY-TWO

The studio. Sarah sits and Turner checks a book for a quote. Sarah knits, heavily pregnant.

Sarah She's kicking.
  What are you reading?

Turner Pope.

Sarah We could go to the Vauxhall Gardens tomorrow. If it's nice.

Turner I need a few hours in the morning.

Sarah We could luncheon there.

Turner Dad'll be doing his Sunday roast.

Sarah Yes.

Turner We could walk. Along the river.

Sarah Will you take your sketchbook?

Turner I thought I might.

Sarah nods, resigned to it. Turner reads his book. Sarah watches him, studies him.

Sarah I'll enjoy the drawings you'll do of me. It will give me time to think.

I dreamt about the theatre last night. There was a man in the wings. And I couldn't see his face. But I could hear his breathing. And then he touched me. He stood behind me. And held me. And I didn't know if it was beautiful or frightening. We sort of became one body. And his breath was all over me. And running through me. And I didn't know whether to stay or go. He was taking me. And I came. In the dream. Very quietly. But violently.

Turner Was he me?

Sarah No.

Turner John?

Sarah No. He was someone else.

Turner kisses Sarah's brow. He puts his hand over her stomach so that he can feel the baby kicking. Sarah puts her hand on his then takes his hand away. Gives him his hand back.

SCENE TWENTY-THREE

The studio. Turner wears a mourning band. He paints.
We watch him, alone for a while. He is full of the
painting, but also of his father, who has died. He lectures,
but to no one.

Turner It's Hannibal. And he's crossing the Alps. There's
sky. And the sun. The men try to . . . shield themselves.
But up against them there is a vast dark cloud. It's about
to crash down. And there's snow. And storm. But beyond
that is a different sky. Beyond. It's white. The sun is God
and it's a battle. Of dark against light. God versus inertia.
Versus degradation. Versus pain. Versus constraint.
Versus lies. And all the . . . Versus convention. Versus
fear. And . . . the light has to win. It does. Win. And it's
beautiful. And violent. It's sublime.

'Dido's Lament' plays as Turner stares at us.
Behind him the vision of 'Hannibal Crossing the
Alps' appears.

Blackout.